I0808211

JR. GRAPHIC MONSTER STORIES

DRAGONS!

STEVEN ROBERTS

PowerKiDS press
New York

Published in 2013 by The Rosen Publishing Group, Inc.
29 East 21st Street, New York, NY 10010

Copyright © 2013 by The Rosen Publishing Group, Inc.

All rights reserved. No part of this book may be reproduced in any form without permission in writing from the publisher, except by a reviewer.

First Edition

Editor: Joanne Randolph
Book Design: Planman Technologies
Illustrations: Planman Technologies

Library of Congress Cataloging-in-Publication Data

Roberts, Steven.
Dragons! / by Steven Roberts.
p. cm. — (Jr. graphic monster stories)
Includes index.
ISBN 978-1-4488-7903-8 (library binding) — ISBN 978-1-4488-8003-4 (pbk.) — ISBN 978-1-4488-8009-6 (6-pack)
1. Dragons—Juvenile literature. I. Title.
GR830.D7R616 2013
398.24'54—dc23

2012001909

Manufactured in the United States of America

CPSIA Compliance Information: Batch # SW12PK: For Further Information contact Rosen Publishing, New York, New York at 1-800-237-9932

Contents

Main Characters

Duke of Carinthia (c. 1200s) In order to **protect** the people, offered a reward to anyone who could kill the Lindworm of Klagenfurt.

Johann, Werner, Gunther, and Sigfried (c. 1200s) Young peasant men who, with the help of the duke, set a trap to kill the vicious Lindworm of Klagenfurt.

About Dragons

- Today visitors will find a huge fountain in the center of the main square in Klagenfurt, Austria. It shows a huge Lindworm dragon with a long, curling tail and large wings. The growling Lindworm faces a statue of the **mythical** figure Hercules. Hercules represents the strength of the brave men who killed the Lindworm.
- People have described the Lindworm differently through the ages. The largest Lindworms are supposedly about 35 feet (11 m) long. They are various shades of green and gray, so their color matches the landscape. Lindworms fly on their huge, bat-like wings. They have large teeth for attacking their victims and some even breathe fire. Their front legs have long, sharp claws for tearing flesh. Lindworms can use their long tails as weapons, hurling them against their **victims**.

Dragons!

I AM SIR GEORGE!
I AM SIR RALPH!
I AM SIR PETER! WE ARE HERE TO **SLAY** THE DRAGON!
AND *I* AM THE LINDWORM OF KLAGENFURT!
THE *WHAT?*
THE LINDWORM OF KLAGENFURT. YOU'VE NEVER HEARD OF IT?
UH . . . NO.

IT IS FROM A *REAL* DRAGON STORY MY DAD TOLD ME. I'LL TELL YOU THE STORY.
"KLAGENFURT IS A TOWN IN THE HILLS OF AUSTRIA.
"DURING THE **MIDDLE AGES**, KLAGENFURT WAS BUSTLING WITH TRADE.

"YET ALL WAS NOT WELL IN KLAGENFURT. IN THE DARK, FOGGY FOREST LIVED A CREATURE KNOWN AS THE LINDWORM.

"THE LINDWORM **TERRORIZED** THE COUNTRYSIDE IN ITS SEARCH FOR FOOD.

"ONE DAY A YOUNG FARMER WENT OUT LOOKING FOR HIS MISSING COW. . . ."
HERTA! HERTA! WHERE ARE YOU?
"HE WAS NEVER HEARD FROM AGAIN."
AHHHHHHH!

"FEAR OF THE LINDWORM SPREAD THROUGHOUT THE COUNTRYSIDE. FARMERS WERE AFRAID TO LEAVE THEIR HOMES.

"HERDERS **ABANDONED** THEIR FLOCKS."
THE LINDWORM!

"PEOPLE STAYED AWAY FROM THE MARKETPLACE.

"THE PROBLEM WAS BROUGHT TO THE ATTENTION OF THE LOCAL DUKE, WHO OWNED ALL THE LAND IN THE REGION."
ALL TRADE HAS STOPPED, MY LORD. PEOPLE ARE AFRAID OF THE LINDWORM. WE CANNOT COLLECT TAXES.

"THIS ANGERED AND FRUSTRATED THE DUKE."
HOW MAY I BE RID OF THIS BEAST?

"THE DUKE OFFERED A HANDSOME REWARD TO ANYONE WHO WOULD CAPTURE OR KILL THE LINDWORM."
WHOEVER KILLS THE LINDWORM WILL RECEIVE MONEY, LAND, AND **PRAISE** FROM THE DUKE!

"MOST OF THE MERCHANTS AND FARMERS WERE TOO AFRAID TO TRY TO KILL THE LINDWORM."
HOW CAN WE FIGHT SUCH A CREATURE? IT WOULD TEAR US TO PIECES!
IT WOULD SURELY KILL US!

"A GROUP OF FOUR BRAVE FRIENDS DECIDED THEY WOULD TRY THE DARING **FEAT**."
DID YOU HEAR, WERNER? THE DUKE WILL GIVE US MONEY FOR KILLING THE LINDWORM.
WE WOULD GET OUR OWN LAND, TOO!
WE WOULD ALSO WIN THE LOVE OF THE PEOPLE AND THE DUKE!

"THEY CAME UP WITH A PLAN AND PRESENTED IT TO THE DUKE."
WELL, AREN'T YOU **CLEVER** FELLOWS! THIS PLAN MAY JUST WORK.

"BASED ON THE PLAN, THE DUKE HAD A LARGE STONE TOWER BUILT IN A CLEARING IN THE MISTY FOREST."

EXCELLENT!

"THE FOUR MEN MET WITH THEIR FRIEND THE VILLAGE BLACKSMITH."
THIS IS A BIG JOB, BUT I CAN DO IT IF THE DUKE WILL PAY.

"THE BLACKSMITH **FORGED** A LARGE CHAIN AND HEAVY HOOK FOR THEM."
BANG!
BANG!

SSSSSS!

"THE FOUR MEN THEN WENT TO SEE A LOCAL HERDSMAN TO BUY A COW."
SEND THE BILL TO THE DUKE.

"THEY SET THEIR TRAP. THEY CHAINED THE COW TO AN IRON RING AT THE BASE OF THE TOWER."
I HOPE THIS HOLDS THE LINDWORM.
IF IT DOESN'T, WE WILL HAVE A BIG PROBLEM.

"THE MOOING OF THE COW COULD BE HEARD THROUGHOUT THE COUNTRYSIDE."
MOOOO!!

"SOON THE LINDWORM APPEARED FROM THE DARK, FOGGY FOREST.

"THE FRIENDS IN THE TOWER WERE ALMOST OVERCOME WITH FEAR AS THE LINDWORM GOT CLOSER.

"THE SIGHT OF THE BEAST WAS TERRIFYING. IT WAS COVERED WITH **SCALES** AND HAD A LONG TAIL. IT HAD EVIL EYES AND FLARING NOSTRILS THAT SNORTED BLACK STEAM.

"THE LINDWORM OPENED ITS MASSIVE JAWS AND SNAPPED UP THE COW IN ONE BITE.
"SUDDENLY THE BEAST LET OUT A PIERCING SHRIEK AS THE HOOK SANK INTO ITS JAW."
SHRIEEEEEEK!

"THE FOUR MEN RUSHED OUTSIDE TO ATTACK THE LINDWORM."
TAKE HIM! HE IS OURS, MEN!
"THE MEN SET UPON THE BEAST WITH THEIR WEAPONS.

"THE LINDWORM FOUGHT BACK, FLAILING FURIOUSLY."
AHHHH!
CRASH!
"THE CREATURE WENT IN FOR THE KILL, BUT ONE OF THE MEN DEALT THE FINAL BLOW.

"AFTER THE LINDWORM'S DEATH, THE PEOPLE OF KLAGENFURT CELEBRATED FOR DAYS AND TRADE ONCE AGAIN **THRIVED**."
THESE FOUR MEN ARE GREAT HEROES AND FRIENDS TO ALL OF US!

"THE TOWN BUILT A STATUE OF THE LINDWORM, WHICH STANDS TO THIS DAY.

"TO SHOW HIS THANKS, THE DUKE HAD A SPECIAL **FORTRESS** BUILT FOR THE FOUR FRIENDS ON THEIR NEW LAND."
THIS IS *OUR* LAND!

SO IS KLAGENFURT A REAL PLACE? DID IT HAVE A REAL DRAGON?
YES, KLAGENFURT IS A REAL PLACE IN AUSTRIA. I BELIEVE THAT THE DRAGON WAS REAL, TOO.
AHHHH!
WHAT IS IT?
THE SMALLEST LINDWORM YOU WILL EVER SEE!

More Dragon Stories

- **Saint George and the Dragon**
  The story of Saint George and the dragon has been told for centuries. At a lake near a small town in Libya lived a dragon. To keep the dragon from attacking them, villagers fed it sheep and even young children chosen at random by lottery. One day a local princess was selected to be the dragon's next victim and was taken to the lake where the dragon lived. Saint George went to rescue her, wounding the dragon with his lance. The dragon did not die but became tame and followed the princess back to town. The people in town were frightened. Saint George vowed to kill the dragon if the villagers would convert to Christianity. They did so, and Saint George then killed the dragon. A church was built on the site where the dragon was killed. From this place arose a spring whose waters cured all diseases.

- **Pitaka and Hotu-puku**
  A legend from New Zealand involves a dragon named Hotu-puku. Travelers began disappearing near the town of Rotorua. Thinking a rival war party was killing them, a group of men went to confront the war party. They were attacked by Hotu-puku and many of them were killed and eaten. Pitaka was a brave man who got a group of warriors together to hunt the dragon. He hung a noose across a trail that the dragon often used. When he saw the dragon, he stepped into the trail as bait. When the dragon rushed at him, it got caught in the noose and strangled itself. The men cut up the dragon, roasted it, and ate a great feast.

Glossary

abandoned (uh-BAN-dund) Left without planning to come back.

collect (kuh-LEKT) To gather together.

feat (FEET) An act of great bravery, strength, or skill.

forged (FORJD) Created, especially something made from metal.

fortress (FOR-tres) A strong place that can be guarded against attacks.

Middle Ages (MIH-dul AY-jez) The period in European history from about AD 500 to about 1450.

mythical (MITH-ih-kul) Based on or described in old stories; not real.

praise (PRAYZ) Saying nice things about someone.

protect (pruh-TEKT) To keep safe.

scales (SKAYLZ) Hard, bony plates.

slay (SLAY) Kill.

taxes (TAKS-ez) Money added to the price of something or paid to a government for community services.

terrorized (TER-uh-ryzd) Filled with great fear.

thrived (THRYVD) Was successful or did well.

victims (VIK-timz) People or animals that are hurt or killed.

Index

Websites

Due to the changing nature of Internet links, PowerKids Press has developed an online list of websites related to the subject of this book. This site is updated regularly. Please use this link to access the list:

www.powerkidslinks.com/mons/drag/